First Less
Lap Steel
by Jay Leach

MW00799998

CD Contents

1 Chapter 2: String Groups
2 Chapter 3: Slide Exercises
3 Chapter 4: Slide Phrases
4 Chapter 5: Playing I,IV,V in different keys
   Plus Octaves – Examples and Slides
5 Chapter 6: Exercises with Slides and String
   Groups
6 Chapter 7: Slide Exercises
7 Chapter 8: Vibrato
8 Chapter 9: Blues – Singles Note Exercises
9 Chapter 10: "Modified Blues"
10 "Modified Blues" performed
11 "Modified Blues" background track only
12 C6th Exercises from Chapter 11
13 Harmonics
14 "Three Blind Mice"
15 "Three Blind Mice" background track only
16 "Wichita Sunrise"
17 "Wichita Sunrise" background track only

MEL BAY

1 2 3 4 5 6 7 8 9 0

Visit us on the Web at www.melbay.com — E-mail us at email@melbay.com

FIRST LESSONS ON LAP STEEL
TABLE OF CONTENTS

Introduction 3

Chapter One 4
    How to Tune
    Good String Gauges
    The Picks (Hot water to adjust thumbpick)

Chapter Two 8
    Holding the Bar/Using correct pressure
    Right Hand Position with Picks
    Picking String Groups

Chapter Three 10
    The Slide
    Slide Exercises
    Slide Exercises with different string groups

Chapter Four 11
    Simple Slide Phrases
    Slide Phrases with different string groups

Chapter Five 12
    Beginning to Make Music
    What does (I), (IV), (V) mean?
    Playing I IV V Chords in different keys
    Octaves
    Octave Slides

Chapter Six 15
    Now the Fun Begins!

Chapter Seven 22
    Slide Exercises to practice playing in tune

Chapter Eight 24
    Vibrato

Chapter Nine 25
    Simple tuning change to play the blues

Chapter Ten 29
    The "Modified Blues"

Chapter Eleven 31
    Back to C6th

Chapter Twelve 32
    Harmonics

Chapter Thirteen 35
    "Three Blind Mice"

Chapter Fourteen 37
    "Wichita Sunrise"

About the Author 39

INTRODUCTION

Thank you for purchasing this book. You are about to learn to play an instrument that is very unique and is sure to provide you with many hours of enjoyment. This instrument is called a **Lap Steel** for the simple reason that it's Steel Guitar that's played while resting on your lap. Its origin is from the Hawaiian Islands around a century ago and from there has evolved from Acoustic to Electric, from 6 to 8 to as many as 14 strings. From the lap on up to Steel guitars with legs so you could stand up and play them, to multiple necks with different tunings, and finally to **Pedal** Steel Guitars where besides playing with picks and a bar individual pedals and levers under the instrument raise and lower certain strings.

For our purposes this book is designed to take you from just being a beginning Lap steel enthusiast to someone who will actually be able make music with the instrument, find some really cool and fun things to play and experiment with, and even jam with friends. Remember persistence and consistency are the keys to learning to do anything and if you apply those qualities to this book and your Lap Steel, you're going to be amazed at your progress. Here's wishing you a fun and exciting new chapter in your musical life.

Sincerely,

Jay Leach

ACKNOWLEDGEMENTS

As with all the projects I have ever done, upon completion you look back and see how many people contributed their unique gifts and abilities to help make a dream become a reality and this project is no different.

I would like to thank Bill Bay and Collin Bay for another opportunity to work with Mel Bay Publications on yet another project. Josh Buck for his help in production, the best copyist you could ever want, Don McGinnis, great photography from Jonathan Gibby, Nick and the folks at the Mac Store in Northridge, CA, my engineer and assistant Aaron Levy, Gold Tone Musical instruments for a great Lap Steel, my wife Pam for her support, and finally our Lord who makes the impossible possible.

Thank you all so much.

Chapter One
How to Tune

Notes in staff of tuning

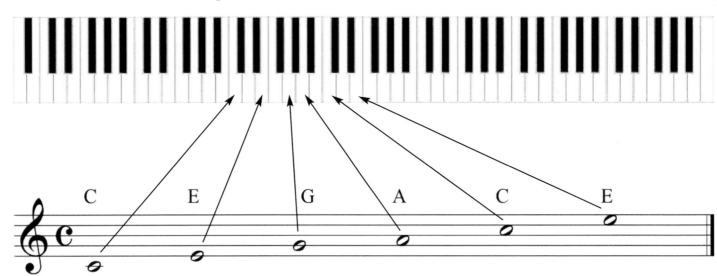

C   E   G   A   C   E

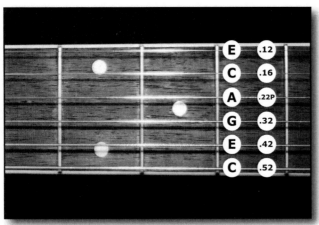

Fingerboard with names of strings and string gauges from the top down.

Needle Tuner

Elixir Strings

Elixir Strings

Bar

Picks

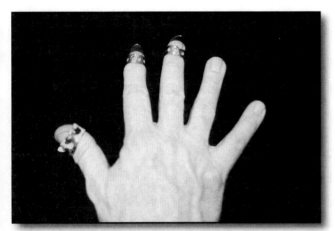

Picks on Hand

Picks on Fingers on Strings

Picks on Fingers on Strings

Bar on Strings (Front)

Bar on Strings (Top)

YOUR PICKS

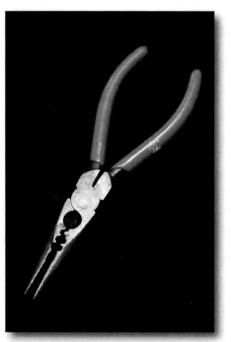

Needle Nose Pliers

Comfortable picks are really important to enjoy playing the Steel Guitar—just ask any Steel player. In my own case when I get a set of picks that feel great I guard them with my life. I have a little plastic thing I put them in then I put that in a plastic box and then I put **that** in a compartment of the seat that I sit on that has storage inside. You don't have to get that nutty but once you get them right just keep 'em in a safe place. I recommend metal finger picks and a plastic thumb pick and so here's what you do: with needle nose pliers make a series of little bends in the part of the pick that goes around your finger to form fit it to your finger so it's snug but **not too tight**. Keep tweekin' till it feels good and if you mess up and have to start over with a new pick—no big deal. On the part of the pick that addresses the string between and 1/4 to 3/8th of an inch from the circular part bend it up to approx. 90 degrees (see illustration). This will ensure your picks are hitting the strings at the right angle so that you will have proper right hand technique.

Bending the Round Part

Bending the Straight Part

Thumb Pick

Buy several thumbpicks because it's always good to have a couple of spares and hopefully one will fit just right. In the event they don't here's a little tip I learned long ago. Just get some hot (not boiling) water, put it into a bowl, throw in your thumb pick for about 30-45 seconds, and when you take it out you'll see it's easy to bend into shape for a good fit around your thumb. Let it cool off and it should fit great.

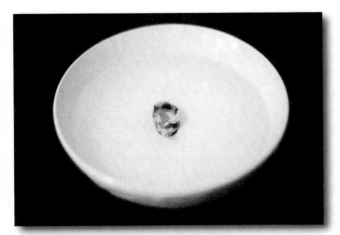

Bowl with Pick in it

Thumb with Pick on it

7

Chapter Two
Holding the Bar/Using Correct Pressure

Holding the bar correctly is very important to the tone and intonation of the Lap Steel. The bar should be held between the index and 2nd finger of the left hand and it's alignment should be **exactly** parallel with the fret markers on the neck of your Steel. If it's not exactly in alignment with the fret marker you **will** be out of tune. As far as the pressure required all you need is a little firm pressure. Not enough pressure will produce one of the most annoying sounds ever heard by human ears and too much will result in stretching the strings producing a different kind of "out of tune." You'll feel it by finding a happy medium and it will quickly become comfortable.

Bar out of alignment.

String Groups

This will be your first introduction to the different string groups on the instrument but it will be something you **always** incorporate in your Lap Steel playing. As you play these different groups of strings together really pay attention to the difference in how each group sounds. The number in the circle represents the string and the number in the box is the finger you use to play it.

1 2 3

2 3 4

4 5 6

1 2 4

2 3 5

| C6 or Amin | C6/5 or Amin7 | C | C | C6 |

Chapter Three
The Slide

Learning to control the bar with your left hand and slide the bar smoothly is essential to playing the Lap Steel. Here are a couple of exercises using simple slides along with different string groups for you to begin learning to control the bar.

Ex. 1   Strings 1, 2, 3 up 1 fret 2nd fret to 3rd fret
EX. 2   Strings 1, 2, 3 up 3 frets 2nd fret to 5th fret

Different string groups and how they sound with a slide.

Ex. 3A – strings 4, 5, 6 – up 2 frets
　　3B – strings 2, 3, 5 – up 2 frets
　　3C – strings 2, 3, 4 – up 2 frets

Ex. 4A – strings 4, 5, 6 – up 3 frets
　　4B – strings 2, 4, 5 – up 3 frets
　　4C – strings 2, 3, 4 – up 3 frets

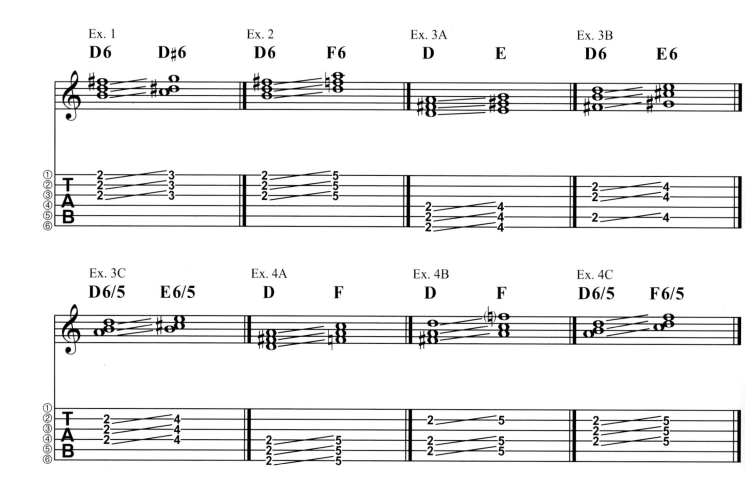

Chapter Four
Three Simple Phrase Ideas

The technical definition of a phrase in musical terms is a note or group of notes that form a natural division of a melodic line. Simply put, it can be a little slur or slide or a simple natural sounding change in the rhythm or syncopation. Phrasing is really important in music as it brings expression, personality, and vitality to a performance. Here are 3 examples of simple phrase ideas you can do sliding only 1 fret that will begin helping you learn to control the bar.

EX. 1 – 323-3
EX. 2 – 3323-3
EX. 3 – 3232323

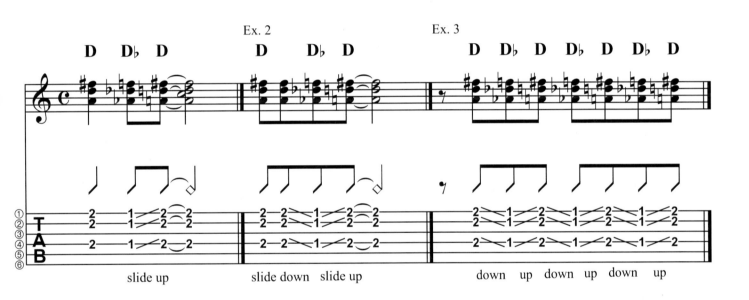

Chapter Five
Beginning to Make Music

What does (I) (IV) (V) mean?

One , Four, Five (always written in roman numerals), refers simply to the location in a scale that a certain note or chord is found. For example in a C scale the notes are: C,D,E,F,G,A,B,C. One (I) refers to the 1st note in the scale or C. Four (IV) refers to the 4th note F and Five (V) refers to G. In a major scale there is a half step between the 3rd and 4th degree and 7th and 8th degree of a scale. Without getting too complicated the way this translates to the Lap Steel is this:

C is the open strings. C♯ is the 1st fret, (½ step up) D is the 2nd fret, D♯ is the 3rd fret, E is the fourth fret and drum roll please...F is our Four, 4, (IV) chord (notice there was on 1 fret between E & F). On up we go to the 6th fret which is F♯ and finally to the 7th fret which is our Five, 5, (V) chord. Now let's look at what's happened: we went up 5 frets to go from the ONE (I) chord C to the FOUR (4) chord F and up 2 more frets to go to the FIVE (5) chord.

See a pattern developing? It's simply: from (I) to (IV) go up 5 frets (I) to (V) go up 7 frets so here's magic formula for Lap Steel (I) (IV) (V) in C as far as fret numbers go is simply 0 (C) + 5 = (F) + 2 = (G)

NOTE: (I)(IV)(V) in ANY key is simply 5 frets up from where you're starting and then 2 more frets up from there for your(V) chord.

Examples: (I)(IV)(V) in D=2-7-9 E=4-9-11 G=7-12-14 and so it goes.

Let's play some examples in the key of D starting on the 2nd fret:

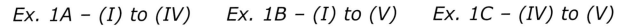

Ex. 1A – (I) to (IV)   Ex. 1B – (I) to (V)   Ex. 1C – (IV) to (V)

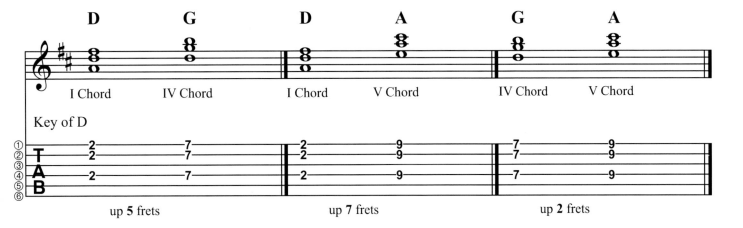

Ex. 2A (I), (IV), (V), (I)   Ex. 2B – (I), (IV), (V), (I)

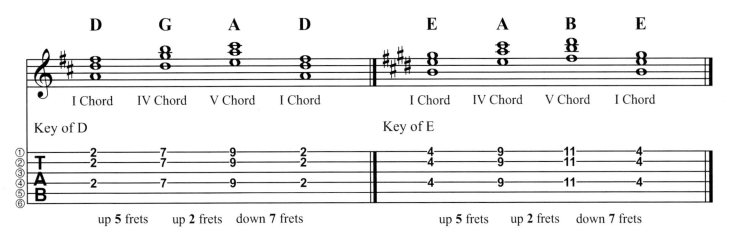

Ex. 2C – (I), (IV), (V), (I) – Key of C   (I), (IV), (V), (I) – Key of G

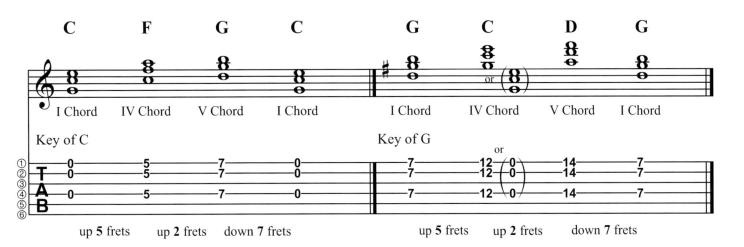

What is an Octave?

An octave is the shortest distance between a given note and it's repetition (or same note) in an ascending or descending series. It can also be defined as a note with twice the oscillation frequency of the same note.

Example: C C♯ D D♯ D E F F♯ G G♯ A A♯ B C

Example of how it looks musically:

In this first exercise we will play several examples of Octaves at different locations up and down the neck. This will also help you become familiar with how an octave sounds. This will also help you get acquainted with playing the 1st and 5th strings or 2nd and 6th strings together.

Ex. 3A Octaves

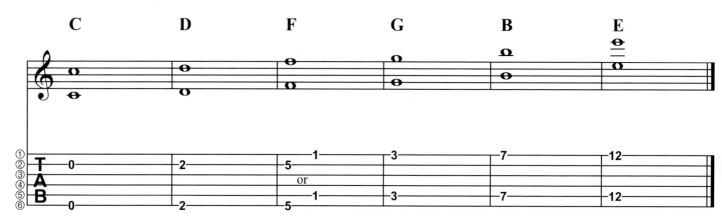

On Lap Steel it is always exactly 12 frets (or 12 1/2 steps) above (or below when possible) any note or group or group of notes you are playing.

Let's practice some 1 octave slides:

Ex. 3B Octaves

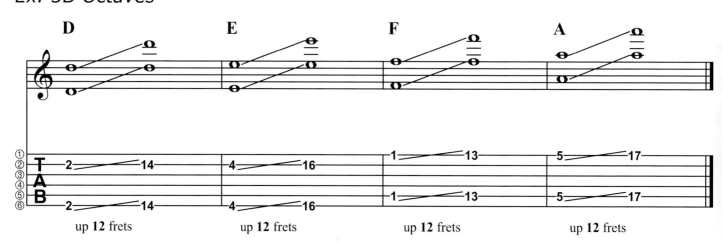

14

NOTE: A cool little trick that's easy to play and that you hear often in Hawaiian music is to slide up 11 frets and then 1 more fret to the octave. This works great for endings!

Example in D:

Ex. 3C Cool Hawaiian Slide

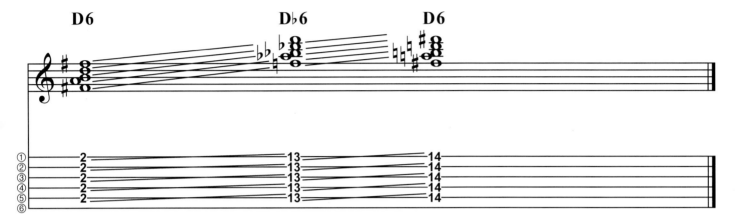

Chapter 6
Now the fun begins!

At this point you have learned what (I),(IV),(V), means, you know what an octave is and you've learned the different string groups. You're moving right along.

The following examples we're going to do are in the key of D (2nd fret as you know). The reason we're going to do these in the key of D is because being up 2 frets will give us a little room for bar control and the ability to slide into our (I) chord. Let's get started!

Ex. 1. Real straight

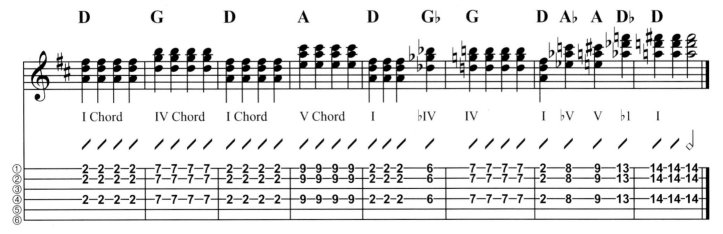

Note: *Adding a dot behind a note increases it's value by 1/2 so a dotted half note gets 3 beats.*

Ex. 2. Not so straight

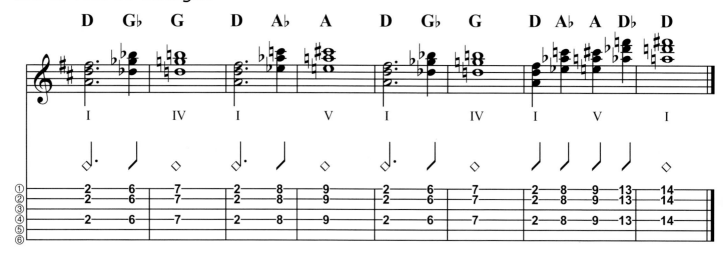

Ex. 3. The same rhythm with different string groups.

Ex. 4. More of the same rhythm with different strings groups and a one octave slide.

Ex. 5. Another new rhythm and notice bars 5 and 7. In bar 5 we're implying a 7th chord with using just 2 strings moving down 2 frets. In bar 7 we're moving down 2 frets using 6ths (See Chap 11) to "imply" a 7th and set up our ending chord.

Ex 6. Here we're playing a combination of the rhythms we've learned along with different string groups and our first use of a minor chord in bar 6.

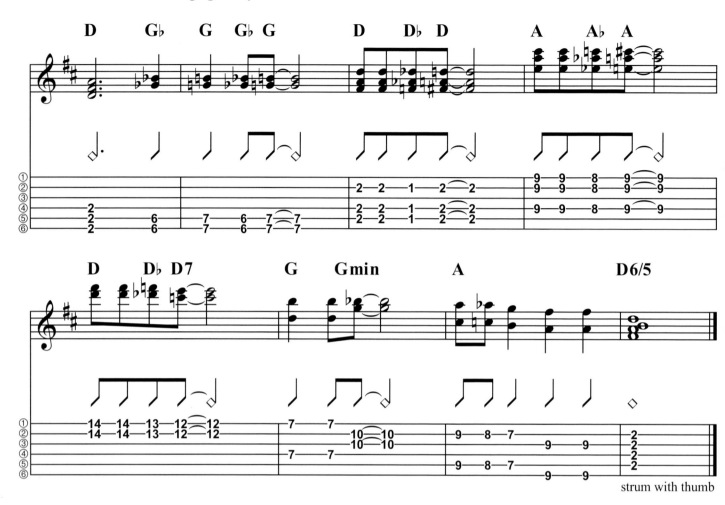

strum with thumb

EX 6A. MAJOR AND MINOR CHORDS!

It's very important to learn about and be aware of major and minor chords both sonically and musically. A major chord consists of the 1st, 3rd, & 5th note in the scale of ANY chord. In a C major chord we have 1 (C) D, E, (3) F, G (5). In a minor chord the 3rd is always flatted so our E becomes E♭. On Lap Steel we play major and minor chords by using different string groups or by slanting the bar. At this point let's just focus on string groups and this little formula for quickly finding the minor chord in relation to the major.

Notice in bar 6 of the above exercise that we go from a major chord to a minor chord and also notice that it's up 3 frets from the major chord. As this next example will show, a good formula in the C6th tuning for going from a major chord to a minor chord is simply "up 3 down 1." "Up" 3 frets and "down" 1 string. Here are three quick examples of major to minor chords for you to really understand this before we move on.

Major to Minor Chords

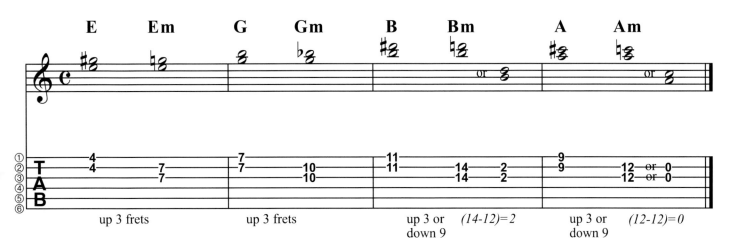

Ex. 7A. An easy "Boogie Woogie" rhythm using different string groups.

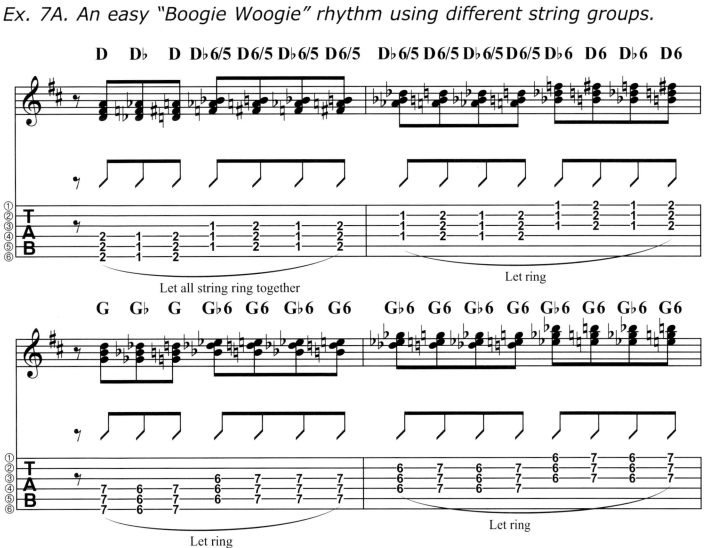

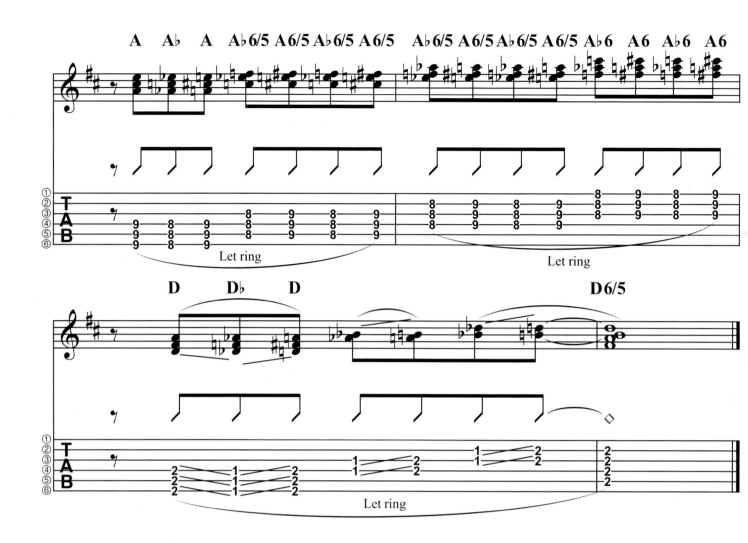

Ex. 7B. The same "Boogie Woogie" exercise we just played but this time we're gonna let the bar do the work. Pick **only** the first group of notes in the phrase as you move through the string groups (you'll notice a P underneath the first group of notes in each phrase). Not only does this sound cool, it will really help you with your bar control.

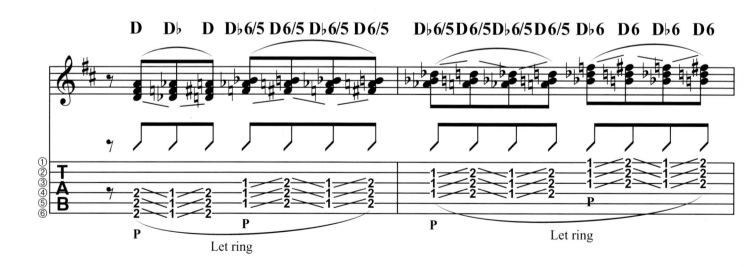

Chapter Seven
Slide Exercises

Playing in tune is absolutely essential to making good music. For anyone playing a fretless instrument it all comes down to a combination of feel, eye, and ear and if you're visually impaired your ear will learn to compensate for your eye. These exercises will not only help you with your hand/eye/ear coordination but it will also serve as one more exercise to help your bar control.

Ex. 1. One Fret Sides

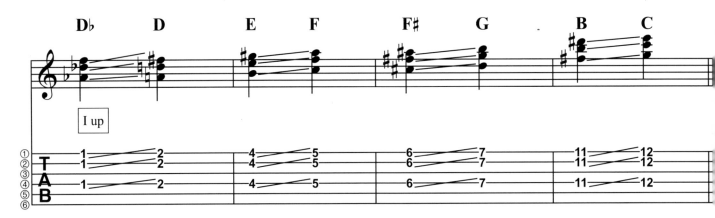

Ex. 2. 3-Fret slides

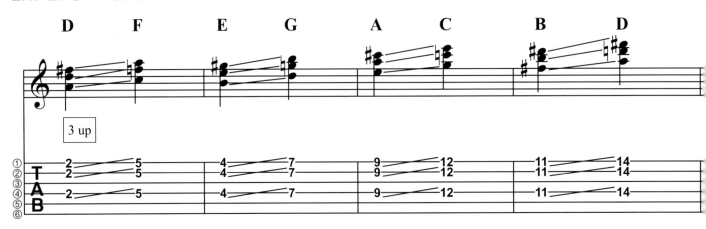

Ex. 3. 3 Frets up 1 Fret down in one motion

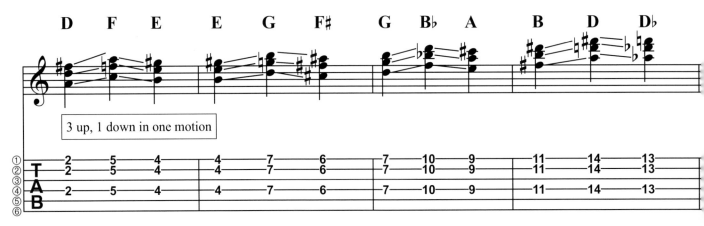

Ex. 4. 5 Frets Up

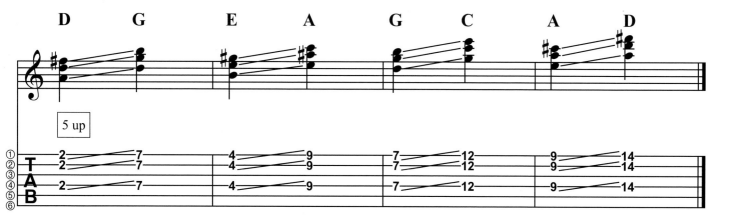

Ex. 5. 3 Frets Down

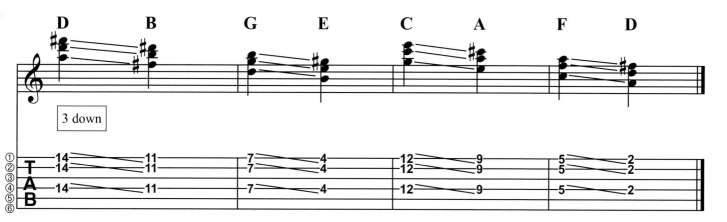

As you begin to get comfortable with this practice all the exercises here with different string groups and different string group combinations. For example: strings 123 up and 235 down etc.

Chapter Eight
Vibrato

Vibrato adds an extra dimension of finesse and beauty to a Steel player's playing in much the same manner as a beautiful vibrato enhances a singer's vocal performance.

There are 2 kinds of vibrato: **Rolling** *and* **Sliding**

The rolling type of vibrato is produced by rolling the bar slightly over the particular fret. The other style is sliding the bar 1/4 to 3/8ths of an inch back and forth. As you will see the different characteristics of vibrato have to do with the **speed** *of the vibrato and* **how much** *or* **how little** *you roll or slide the bar. As you will find, vibrato can go from being very beautiful and lyrical, to making you sound like you're either a nervous wreck or a drunk on New Year's eve. Listen to the recorded examples and in your own trial and error you will find that "happy medium" for something that sounds natural to your ear.*

Chapter Nine
A New Tuning!

By now you have acquired some of the basic skills to play the Lap Steel so le'ts have some fun. We're gonna play the blues and we're going to do it with a very simple change in our tuning. Retune your 3rd string (A) up 1/2 step to Bb. Now instead of being tuned to C6th you're tuned to C7 and you will notice the sound of your Steel went from "sweet and innocent" to "hip and cool"–let's face it, you've probably never heard a "sweet and innocent" blues…that is, until you purchased this book…OK, let's get to work. Remember back in chapters 5 & 6 how you learned about (I)(IV)(V), now you're really gonna see it come to life.

This is what you call a 12 bar blues!

Again we'll do it in the key of D for ease of playing and the form will look like this:

(I), (IV), (I), (I)
(IV), (IV), (I), (I)
(V), (IV), (I), (I)

Ex. 1 Blues

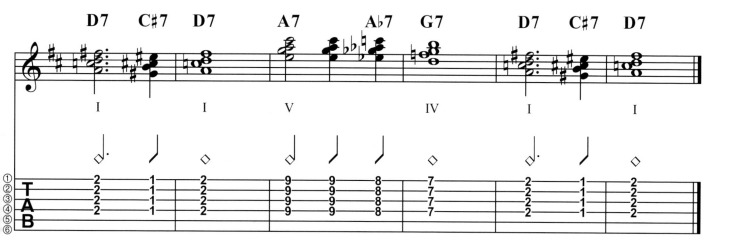

25

You'll notice 1/2 step slides from the (I) chord to the (IV) chord on the 4th beat of the 1st bar to the 2nd, and almost all the bars to follow. This is done to make it more musically fun and interesting.

A Single Note Pattern

Now we are going to add a simple single note pattern that you can use in conjunction with chords in the above exercise. This will be something that you can not only have fun playing but will be fun to use when jamming with friends. Here's the pattern:

Ex. 2

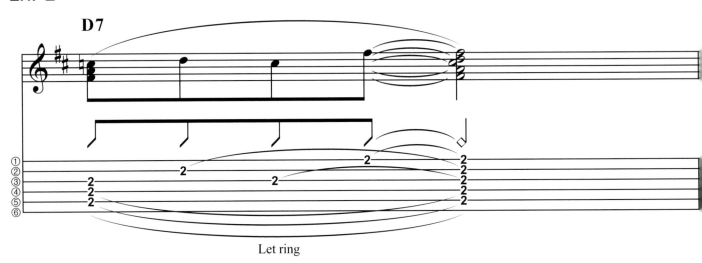

Let ring

Now let's take this pattern that we have just learned and turn it into a simple little (I),(IV),(V) blues.

Ex. 3

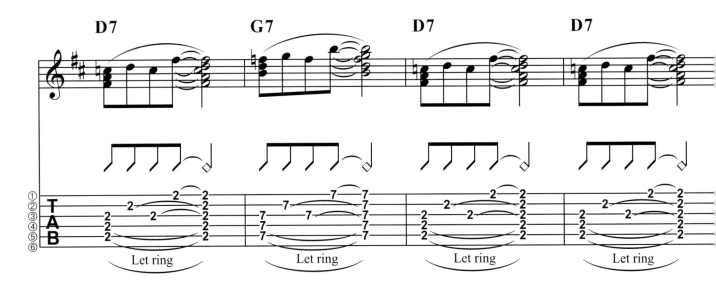

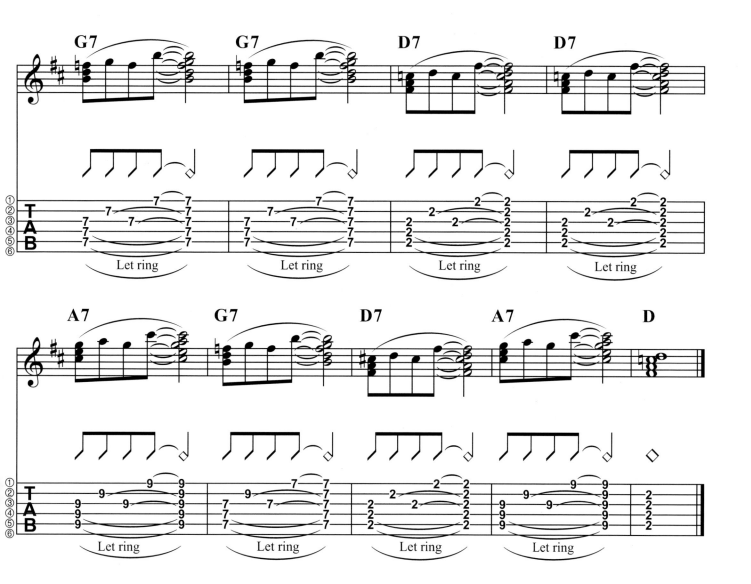

This next exercise is something else that is going to help you continue to grow as a Lap Steel player. It is one of the foundational right hand picking techniques that all Steel Guitar players use. Practice this slowly **with a metronome** and your speed will gradually and naturally progress. It's probably safe to say that you'll use this for all the rest of the days you play the Lap Steel so let's get started. We're starting on the 4th fret so as you know that means we'll be playing in the key of E.

Ex. 4

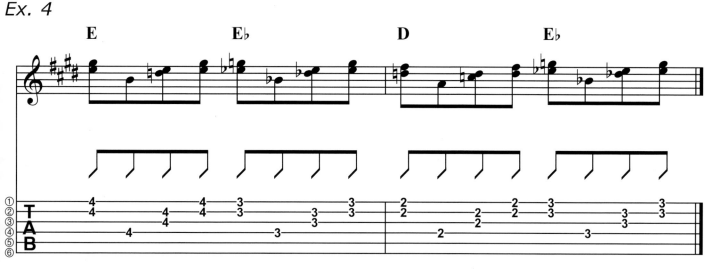

Now notice the difference in the written syncopation. Instead of straight 8th notes you'll notice the dotted 8th-16th combination, this makes the feel swing and kind of skip along.

As you know, straight 8th notes are counted 1&2&3& etc. but as you already know, a dot adds 50% more time value to any note it comes after, so a dotted 8th-16th is counted: one, e, and, **ah**, two, e, and, **ah**, and looks like this:

Ex. 5 Swing Feel

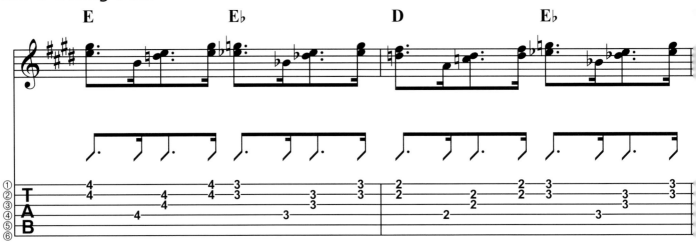

Now add in this new string group on the lower strings in the 2nd bar with the pattern on the top strings that you've just learned and you're going to have a cool little 2 bar phrase. Notice this time there's no Eb chord coming back up. We'll use the new lower string group to resolve you back to E (your (I) chord).

Ex. 6

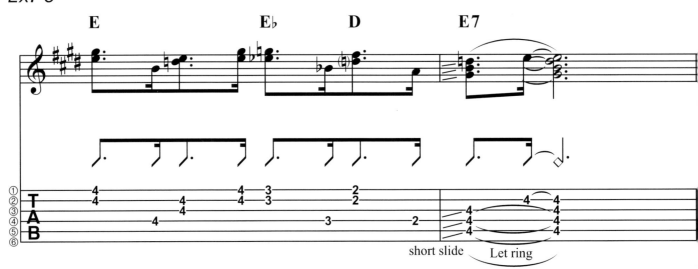

Chapter Ten
"The Modified Blues"

Now let's take this little phrase and make into a simple little "modified" blues. The blues is suppose to make you sad but this one is gonna make you happy! Instead of doing a straight (I) (IV) (V) blues like we've done before, our actual progression is going to be:

(I) (IV) (I) (V) (IV) (III) (II) (bII)

I have recorded this for you with:

A.) A slow, straight, solo, example—boring but you need to hear it.

B.) A little more up tempo solo version—getting there...

C.) A more up tempo version w/ backing track—Fun!

D.) Just the backing track for you to practice with—within minutes you're gonna sound like a famous rock star! See how easy that was...

Ex. 1 "The Modified Blues"

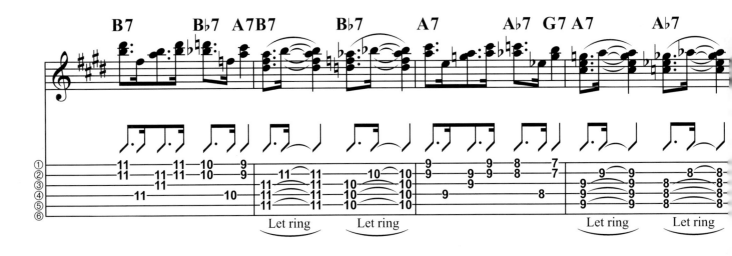

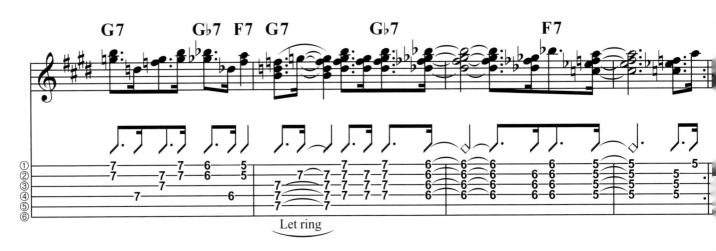

 *"Modified Blues"* performed

 *"Modified Blues"* background track only

Chapter Eleven
Back to C6th

As you begin to grow as a Lap Steel player you will find that it is necessary almost all the time to use different string combinations in different positions to achieve the correct harmony for a song. This is accomplished by using different intervals that contain the correct notes related to the key your playing in regardless of where they are found on the neck.

Here are some examples of different intervals and a simple harmony exercise to illustrate how this works:

Ex. 1

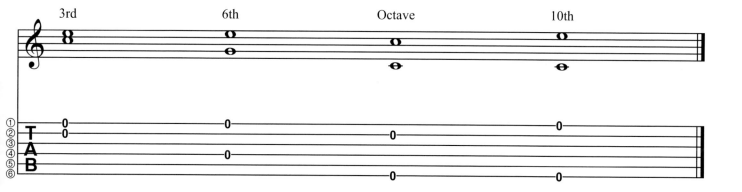

Ex. 2 Harmonized Scale

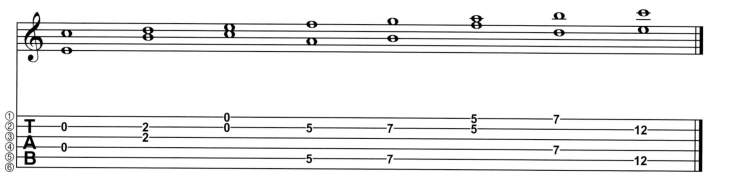

Chapter Twelve
Harmonics

Harmonics are produced when a string is picked with the right hand and touched lightly with the tip of the left finger or side of the left hand at a specific point on the string and then quickly removed. The technical explanation of how and why this happens will be left to scientists to explain in the lunchroom but for our purposes in this book, when this is done correctly it produces a very cool chime effect. Remember earlier in the book when we discussed octaves? An easy way to play open string octaves is to do it with harmonics. Here's what you do: pick an open string and then lightly touch the string with the fingertip of your left hand on the 12th fret. You will hear a chime sound and that sound will be an octave higher than the open string. I have included 2 photos to illustrate playing one note at a time and 1 other photo to show how to lay your fingers across the strings and be able to play different strings at the same time.

Now that you've played some harmonics you know that they really sound cool, (like I mentioned before, kind of like little chimes), now try the same thing you have learned on the 7th then the 5th frets. You will notice that it's a little more difficult but the pitches are really neat and different than just the straight octave on the 12th fret. Now 5 frets **up** from the octave try the same thing (12+5=17th fret) and 12+7=19th fret) (it's OK, I know you don't need a math tutor...)

Now one final thing 12+12=24th fret- It's way up there but it's an easy harmonic to play and it's an octave higher than the one on the 12th fret.

Spend time learning to play crisp, clear harmonics. They're a great thing to have in your musical "tool bag."

Here are some harmonic exercises that will help you practice playing them in different ways.

1.) Going from string to string vertically.
2.) Going back and forth across the neck horizontally between the 7th & 12th fret alternating from string to string.
3.) Playing "cascading" harmonics both ascending and descending.

The easiest harmonics to play are found on the 12th fret so let's begin with vertically alternating strings.

Ex. 1

Next let's alternate between the 12th and 7th fret on the same string as we descend and notice that our last harmonic is on the 5th fret on the 6th string. Pay particular attention to the pitches that these harmonics make as you never know when you might be able to incorporate them in a song.

Ex. 2

Ex. 3 Cascading Up

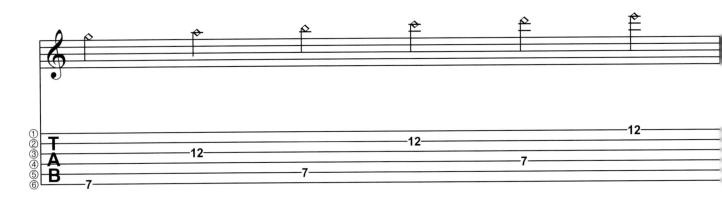

Ex. 4 Cascading Down

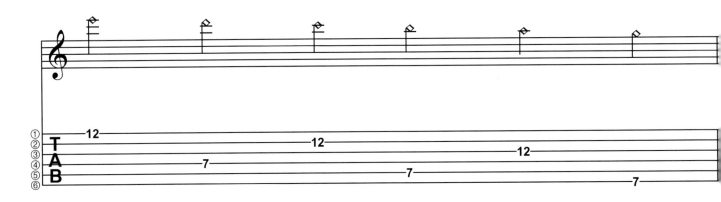

Chapter Thirteen
"Three Blind Mice"

Three (really) Blind, (but pretty hip), Mice. I don't know much about these mice but I do know their song just got a major makeover....

This is a simple little song that everyone knows but it will serve as a perfect example of little things you can do as a musician to take something from boring and mundane to interesting, fun, and unpredictable. Let's dissect this arrangement: the first bar is just the simplest single line melody played on one string. The second is the melody restated in 6ths (that's the name of the musical intervals of the notes). The third bar is the melody in 3rds and the 4th is the melody implied with a little lick that's close to the melody. Notice the same similarity in bars 5, 6, 7, then the most recognizable part of the melody played in bars 8 & 9. Now notice the second ending, the chord is not what you expect to hear but notice this: the final note of the melody (E), is the top note of the new chord. This is what is known as a "deceptive cadence ending." This is a time honored mechanism that composers use to add intrigue and interest to music. The chord I found here sounds really cool because of the open E and C (the ♭7th and the 9th of the chord) open strings combined with the bar covering the bottom 4 strings on the second fret (a D6 chord). All this as you again restate the chord by playing (called arpeggiating) the single notes in the chord and then doing a smooth slide up to resolve to the "real" ending chord. By the way, just because you're a beginning Lap Steel player that doesn't mean you can't do some different fun things that are easy to play. This ending is a great example of something that happens throughout music (and life also), tension/resolution.

Three (like really) Blind (like pretty hip) Mice

Chapter Fourteen
Wichita Sunrise

I have many great memories from Wichita mornings and so I wrote a happy little song that I hope will not only be fun for you to play but also incorporate many of the things you have learned in this book.

Beginning with the 2nd chord we see something really cool. If we place the bar over just three of the strings (2, 3, 4) and leave the top string open we get a chord that not only has a really unique sound but also cannot be played anywhere else or any other way on the Lap Steel (by the way, the name of the chord is F#9).

Next remember when we learned earlier how minor chords are are played 3 frets up from major chords so check out measures 3 & 4, and measures 5 & 6. Notice in bars 7 & 8 how that as the chords go down after C we run out of room and have to go UP an octave to compensate. No big deal, it's a common occurrence on Lap Steel. Finally notice in bars 9 & 10 we slide down 2 frets from our Major chord. This is a great way as we've mentioned to "imply" the 7th when playing a major chord.

I hope you have enjoyed this book and gained some valuable insights into this great little instrument and also into the wonderful world of music. I wish you God's richest blessings in all of your future musical endeavors.

Sincerely,

Jay Leach

Wichita Sunrise

About the Author

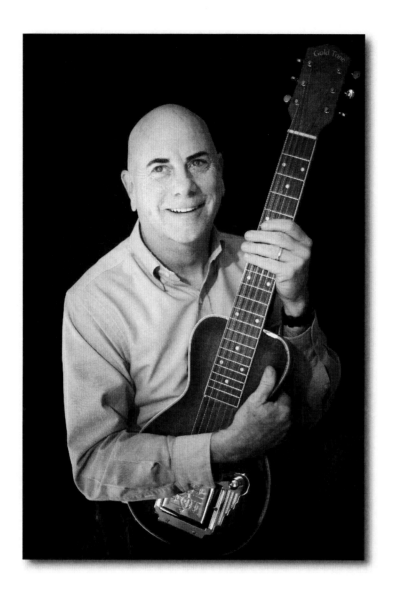

Jay Leach has been a freelance studio musician in Los Angeles for many years. As a multi-instrumentalist he has worked on numerous motion picture soundtracks, television shows, jingles, and live performances including a performance with the Los Angeles Philharmonic in 2011. Among his other freelance work he has been the Pedal Steel Guitarist for the TV show "American Idol" since 2006.

In addition to Jay's work as a professional musician in Los Angeles he also has a career as a solo artist. As a guitarist Jay has contributed to 2 Mel Bay collection books, "Portraits of Christmas" and "Fingerstyle Anthology 2000" and has his own Mel Bay book of fingerstyle guitar originals entitled "Contemporary Christian Fingerstyle Guitar." As an artist Jay has 7 CDs and tours on a limited basis doing concerts in the US and Canada. For more information visit Jay on Facebook or Twitter or at: www.JayLeach.com or on YouTube at JayLeachMusic.